Mosaicq

poems by

Kitty Jospé

Finishing Line Press
Georgetown, Kentucky

Mosaicq

Copyright © 2013 by Kitty Jospé
ISBN 978-1-62229-375-9 First Edition
All rights reserved under International and Pan-American Copyright Conventions. No part of this book may be reproduced in any manner whatsoever without written permission from the publisher, except in the case of brief quotations embodied in critical articles and reviews.

ACKNOWLEDGMENTS

Grateful acknowledgement is made to the editors of the following publications in which the following poems have appeared:

Poet Talk : Monthly Publication of **Just Poets**, Rochester, NY: 2010: *On Silk Road*

Centrifugal Eye: 2011: *For the time being, Mona Lisa says* (April/May: April is the Cruelest Month: A Bitter Point of View. p. 62) 2012: *Somewhat After Machado* (Winter Holiday: Nose like a Cherry: Scents & Sense Memories p. 27.)

Grasslimb: 2012: Vol. 9, No. 2: *Janus Slipping on His Other Face*

Liberty's Vigil, The Occupy Anthology. Foothills Publishing, January 2012: *The Word of the Day*

Nimrod: Spring 2011: Vol. 54, No. 2 (Growing Season p. 14): *When the sun shines...*

Redactions: Issue 14: 2011 (The I-90 Poetry Revolution, p. 30): *The Wanting Urge*

Poetrybay.Com: Winter 2012-13: http://www.poetrybay.com/: *Setting Moon Table*

Le Mot Juste 2012: A Poetry Anthology by Members of Just Poets, Foothills Publishing. 2012: *Falling*

Editor: Christen Kincaid
Cover Photo: Timothy J. Fuss/Mary-Louise Gerek
Author Photo: Timothy J. Fuss

Printed in the USA on acid-free paper.
Order online: www.finishinglinepress.com
   also available on amazon.com

Author inquiries and mail orders:
Finishing Line Press
P. O. Box 1626
Georgetown, Kentucky 40324
U. S. A.

TABLE OF CONTENTS

Tiles over Time
2. Mosaic – detail of the Three Kings
3. Janus Slipping on His Other Face
4. When the sun shines on the window pane in spring
5. Somewhat after Machado
6. Spring Cleaning
7. Almost then not any more
8. Word Pottery
9. Nursing Home

Piecing Faces
10. Along the Silk Road
11. A Taste of Collelugno
12. Da Capo al Fine
13. What Flies
14. For the time being, Mona Lisa says

Mother Remains
15. Disconnected
16. Diptych
17. The Linen
18. Not Yet Crossing the River Styx
19. Our Weekly Letters
20. Falling
21. Setting Moon Table

Choosing Tesserae
22. The Wanting Urge
23. Spring Stage – Dent-de-Lion
24. Happy New Year Nonetheless
25. Recipe
26. Word of the Day
27. Teal in Spring

MOSAICQ: c.1400, from O.Fr. mosaicq "mosaic work," from M.L. musaicum "mosaic work, work of the Muses". Mosaic is the art of creating images with an assemblage of small pieces of colored glass, known as tessellae.

It is the gift of the imagination, to imagine what isn't, break what is and piece together the broken into a new whole. The gift of shared creativity binds this book from the cover of the art quilt created by Mary Louise Gerek in response to the final poem. My thanks goes to the countless people who have read and responded to these poems.

Mosaicq – detail of the Three Kings

Hurry! Hurry! Of course you must
deliver these gifts
of gold, frankincense, myrrh—

if
     someone invented you as
three magi from three continents carrying
temporal, spiritual and healing power—
and if
     it does not matter that wise men
are not mentioned in the gospels—

        we'll still sing carols about you.

Here you are tiled in tights, passion-red hats,
feet scarcely touching the ground—
leaping out of broken bits—
tell us your story—

and why that first rigid angel with a chartreuse halo,
holds a disembodied hand out to you,
stares at us as if to ask
and what gifts do you have—
and what do you hurry to bring?

detail of nave mosaic in Sant'Apollinare Nuovo, Ravenna,
depicting the Three Magi

Janus Slipping on His Other Face

Our two chairs angle toward the window
each of us holding a book
his about inland seas
and mine about potters in the Southwest,
who before disappearing

break a hole in the center of each pot
allowing its spirit
to join them in their burial grounds.

I imagine my father falling that way
through dusky space, as he slips away
from knowing January or memory
of the god in charge of gates,
beginnings, endings.

It is easier to turn to the piano than speak.
The sound is loud enough for him to hear.

I play a piece that dances and trills
without any need of a discernible key.
It ends with a cascade from the highest note
to the lowest.

And then we sit, silence beating.

When the sun shines on the window pane in spring

... it becomes clear
spiders are not losing their hair,
but rather sending unscripted valentines.

Today's unbirthday greeting spun to remind you
that sure as the sun will set,
you are getting older.

It's not words that make it bearable
so much as the swing of the silk,
the dancing in the frame.

Somewhat After Machado

The summer afternoon casts shadows
not ready to move to evening.
Wind tosses the sumac, flounces the hawthorn,
exposes that bare casualty of cornfield,
ripped and barren among shoulder-high stalks.

Do you grieve this gash on Earth's skin?
What if hurt could be wrapped by clouds soft as zero
silent as air caught in an upside-down cup?

A dragonfly helicopters by, stirring the mint of *Malva
neglecta*.
The painted lady has left her eggs there
and you sense her caterpillars
becoming your fingers,
at the very edge of being.
Just then a great idea unshadows,
tumbles into the gap in the cloud spill,
jet-sounds slicing the heat and drumroll
of thru-way hum.

This is when *one* sneaks out of *alone*
like the heady scent of summer lilies
remembered in winter. When *end*
dusts its feet in what has been tended,
shadowed.

Spring Cleaning

The enlarger sits next to the packets of unused film
as if to say once it was the king of the darkroom
able to click shades into form

and the film sits next to the camera
as if to say it once was the magic inside
the camera's inner chamber

and the album of photos creaks between leather covers
as if ashamed to say that all that is left
are a few faded squares of paper.

The images say in cream, sepia or gray,
it was 1902, at the church picnic
and the children were running races

legs caught mid-air
hat ribbons pasted motionless—

and you see your childhood
like a four-year-old clambering over a fence
on a bright spring day where dandelions
sun themselves, promise gold and yet
the bell rings, and you return,
throw away the limp chain you have made
so you won't stain your shirt.

Almost then not any more

It's just
      the unpinable weather,
yesterday, a thumb of crocus
today the rip of gusting white
wrenching limbs off 300 year oak
as unpredictable as my father who says,
life couldn't be better
but who can't handle words any more.

It's just
      winter I write to instead of
my father who told me *don't feel you
have to send any letters any more.*

It's just
      another phone call,
and we start our mobius strip of talk:
he asks, *How's everything*
                I answer, *just fine.*
It doesn't matter what I'd answer.
He'd still say, *that's good—*

so close to *almost,*
so near to *not any more.*

Word Pottery

Ramblers rise to warm rose by
rose as my father etches letters
like so many sheep curls blown
full in the horn. He is an old potter,
staring at pieces of what once seemed
whole,
writing to my mother
as if to unearth a half-buried urn,
still intact after 40 silent years.
He rubs the burin to form unbroken
lines, to contradict the shards
of their story.

He looks up, asks what she wants to hear.
Word by word,
he works memory,
kneads letter by letter.
How's that? he says to me,
showing three trembling lines—

soundless syllables
rinds of rooms without doors.

Nursing Home: diary entry

Night:
a small ragdoll of a woman shrieks in her room
her hospital nightie
tied by a loose band at the back of her neck.
It could be you,
or me,
or a bad dream in Baghdad
where you feed silver into a phone's belly
but cannot connect and a bomb sends
you inside a
collapsed coal mine shaft.

I wheel her to her the bathroom,
help her to the throne,

       help her back to the wheelchair,
smooth wisps of white hair off her withered cheeks.

She moans, *please let me go home.*
I hold her head, kiss her hands.

I want to go home she cries.

I hold her shoulders gently, but tight.
This is me. This is you.

*Along the Silk Road – Cleave Poem**

The job description,	to complicate
speak a new language	to make a new world
voice	like spinning silk
woven from the soul	threaded heart to heart
half to understand	halved,
have is illusion;	just as oneness,
otherness	belongs
in each separate part	to the Belovèd
like the man searching	a lost son. Do you know
	how the father,
do you know how he	found him?
discovered his lost son?	The man thought
each person,	*whoever comes before me*
he thought, *This could be him,*	*This could be him.*

*In a cleave poem, you can read each vertical column separately,
then the third time, read them together horizontally.

A Taste of Collelugno

We are offered, here in Collelugno,
a taste of homemade pear grappa,
a slice of prosciutto,
a generous *try this*
at the *negozio di alimentari*.
It allows us to see
beyond what we think we see
here in Collelugno
whose name means simply,
what lies on a rise of a hill.

The shopkeeper steps away from his counter,
tells us to follow him past the series of stone houses
to his pear trees beyond the church tower
the very ones pictured on the label
of the bottle of grappa.

We take a picture of him,
his orchard,
the bottle,
the church tower,
buy it all
to allow us once again
a taste
of Collelugno.

Da Capo al Fine

Nothing to fear but...
the split-bellied gutter gushing
pounds and pounds of water
where it shouldn't

this too shall...
fix nothing, as lighting takes giant steps
down the trembling plum

don't ...
worries itself into the conversation
like embroidery thread whose gnarled knots
hide on the underside.

Nothing to fear,
say I, stitching a small tear
in a pillow case hem we've had for 40 years,

Everything's fine, I say
just fine, says he
and we mumble Dharma reminders
until it's believable
like otherworldly sunlight shifting—

fine.

What Flies

The law of matrimony applies the usual *how did you sleep?*
But there is no answer.

Dawn hinges heavy with haze as if too hot to unwrap
its pinked edges while a plump fly snarls
against a screen, stopping only to clean and buffer
its silvery wings.

The law of parsimony says to swat—
one less disease-carrying housefly's nattering.
The law of kindness says to push open the screen
and let it buzz into the sultry day.

My man rises,
silent,
intent,
releases the hinge-clasp
      removes the screen,
         wields it like a shield
             and our intruder
                flat-hats
                    out the window

and dawn lightens.

For the time being, Mona Lisa says,

*I'll ignore
the crack in the sky above my head.*
She is painted on poplar, famous
enough for someone to dovetail the back,
popular enough for people to care
to prevent the wormholes from widening.

Tell me, she says, *what you think lies
behind my smile?* She is caught,
like a mouse in a world
layered in brown ochre,
imagination above her.

It's April in Paris, and she remains
in her museum frame. How many ask her
questions? Isn't her smile the requisite polish
used to hold ourselves together?

Like the man on the podium, giving a speech.
No one guesses that his son is one of the survivors,
as well as the soldier who shot himself. Or the woman who turns
the corners of her mouth into a pleasant vacancy,
alluding to changing jobs. Or the museum guard
from Peru telling a JewelRed-26-lipsticked docent
you have a lovely sonrisa.
Mona's message seals back: *I'm just fine*
regardless of the crack above her head.
Her lips play a trap for *une souris,*
the French for mouse.

What if she believes that is the only way
to engage in a real conversation?

Disconnected

Picasso paints my insides
with the outsides
of his weeping woman:
her violet, cobalt, tourmaline hair
sweeps to jigsaw colors
cutting deep.

White skewers, green clamps,
blue creases, purple, yellow
pleat her face into angles that say
don't touch.

Such a lonely place.

I want to ask her if she is clenching
her handkerchief to express grief
or if those three green fingers,
two yellow eyes of fingernails,
that jagged white stovepipe
of a thumb repress it.

What rips at a mind like that?

Energy weeps in colors chiseled
into shapes—they
cut the chords in the throat.

Diptych: Inspired by, Peter Paul Rubens, The Head of the Medusa.

I
Even after Medusa's head was severed,
Rubens knew how to keep the magic—
her mad eyes still ready to turn you to stone
as blood writhes out of her neck
where sinew and snake twist together
knotted and ravenous—

and so we avert our look.

II
I do not avert my look but study
my mother's eyes.
They do not say *Merry Christmas,*
she is too honest to say that.
Nor do her eyes glare with the fury of Medusa
as they once did.
She is looking up from the picture book
I made for her of snapshots that witness time
she was not gorgon at all.

Her eyes are bright as Alpheratz,
the star Arabian astronomers call
Head of the Woman in Chains.

If she were Medusa, my heart
would not be such a clenched fist
aching to be turned to stone.

*The Linen**

If you ask the maid
she will tell you
the lady, skinny as a nail
is ghosting

and the lady, will tell you
the maid has scrubbed her and the sheets
to bare threads, wind host.

Leaves drip above
the lady's head, and the turquoise sky
is chill in the distance. No sting

in the wheat, nor braised brick roofs.
Nothing in this garden is really
about the garden, nor is there a hollow

ting of a bell on the gate
or visitor or understanding
of whatever is no longer, washed
and now shrouded in the threads,
drying, rising up, to free her
ghosting.

* after the painting, *The Linen* by Pierre Bonnard, 1909

Not Yet Crossing the River Styx

What I know of hell and riddles
(hidden in the curve of each granite drop
of pomegranate)
I have learned from my mother.

As a young girl, I watched her spirited
away from the summer of her motherhood,
repeatedly not quite returning year after year.
You too would mourn losing such
perfume of lilies, laughter of cornstalk in the wind,
coltish sense of humor.

If we had known then about elastic words
beak—air—full
it might have eased the terror, weight of grief.
Be careful !
(beaks of orchid become octopus rostrum
suckered arms, strangling in the deep.)

Let us be clear about fearful.
Change of season, repeats again and again
whatever fill of care.

We know the offer of ruby seeds,
We know of Persephone,
beyond the Styx without her mother's embrace.

But imagine it the other way around.
The daughter watches her mother carried off,
apple blossom just in bloom.

Now it is autumn, the sun springing over the hill,
sparkling the morning frost,
and I gently squeeze those hard blood-red drops
of *Pomum granatus,* seeded apple,
as if to press tenderness deep into living.
Words crumble like papery moth.

Our Weekly Letters

Her tiny script claws a lobster parade
of words repeating fact:
clothes: rifled
puzzle: pieces stolen
toilet: clogged again with three rolls of paper
activities: canceled
coffee: suspect, diluted or forgotten.
Ice cream: a real treat

Enclosed for the fifth time
her roommate's *promise note to pay
ten million dollars.*
No explanation.

This is my mother's world.

Thousands of raw hours we have written.
We use our letters like bait
to catch pieces of ourselves,
signing oceans
with mermaid tails.

Falling

I want to remember the things
my mother loved –
give her a singing kettle
for something better than instant Yuban.

Only a vague idea remains of her two string basses
bowing out of cases,
belting and buzzing as they burst into song.
But they too have fallen out of sight,
gone now,
along with the clutter of shells
      (painstakingly mounted fifty years ago)
her old books collected in Boston
      (bookshelved in Michigan
          boxed to Atlanta
              blighted by moth, mold in Florida)
and her tennis racquet tossed out along with her days of
coaching,
penned in her *Owed to Tennis.*

It all gallops by past a fragrance of pine
scenting the air seen through the frame of cocked ears
galloping, galloping,
as she rides towards her end,
sliding now—
I reach for the mane,
clutch the sound
echoing
dignity, dignity
whispered until mute...
    dignity

        dignity...

        ...

Setting Moon Table

There's something about the way
the moon's fingernail of light
traces the idea of a jawbone—

it's much more dramatic than
the moon's cratered mask—
something careless
about a caress of the sun in the soundless dark;

Something carefree
about the old moon swinging the new moon in her arms,
as crimson seeps into dawn.

Next week, will you think of looking
for the moon—

will you notice hunger taking its place?

The Wanting Urge

a look in the mirror
    urges the hand to seize the scissors
        cut a bit of brassy highlight out
            temptation clicks on
                that voice saying *I can't*
                stand it
            the desire to tonsure the unnatural
        to seize the blades
    wield them like a scythe to the scalp
a garden *weasel* to the weeds
        and all becomes upheaval
    revolution   fires urgency into a fast-forward swell
        and then it's too late—the scissor jaws eat
                hungry for work
and *urgent* chucks every check
    until it's impossible to expel chaos

        this suddenly intolerable sunlit crown
            heers on the starving scissors.

This time, the woman observes strands of silence
as ragged ends rage into bangs.
Natural takes time to fall
she murmurs,
      into place.

Spring Stage –Dent-de-Lion

Imagine if we didn't call them *weed*
or French *piss-en-lit*, spoiling a green lawn,
but *manes of the King of the Earth*—
imagine, seeing beyond
such crowns.

Instead, you think, *This cluster of toothy leaf*
attached to a deep taproot
must go,
as midway in the earth,
the trowel snaps a branching radix.
Like a hydra, it will have all summer long
to multiply its necks and radicles—
like thoughts you would prefer to thrash
out the door.

Little keeps us going—
etched leaf of jewel weed,
buttercup nod to Queen Anne's Lace in the sprawl.
Babybreath will be white bed straw
brushed by zebra swallowtail

and the thought of summer breathes
high time crowned
in seeded heat.

Happy New Year Nonetheless

In the kitchen, my Flemish husband
is reading a new year's card: *Ongelooflijk* !
he says outloud, which sounds sticky,
like French fingernails holding a loofa,
scrubbing away the unwanted.

Something like hit the road Jack
On geloof lijk, don't you come back no more.

The card is talking about family life,
personal experiences in a jocular way
the Dutch *unbelievable* capturing an upbeat,
energetic tone.
No commentary on politics,
disasters, injustice, wars but a simple
Onaanvaardbaar! which might sound
like a hardened aardvark to non Dutch-speakers.

Repeat *On-aan- vaardbaar* to work
this form of unacceptable on the tongue
like Dutch taffy.

It reminds me of our high school mascot—
an aardvark made of brown papier-maché.
There's a certain similarity between
the use of mascots and news in review.
Imagine any opposing team
seeing our foot-digging, nocturnal
earth pig with unfortunate teeth!

It makes more sense to me than jags of world news
javelined to strike keyboards, screens,
virtual scenes outside my ken.
Who decides what
in this land *of, for, by* the people.
And so quickly.

I say, slow down HappyNewYear—
and see that aardvark
chase *onaanvaardbaar* away.
Ongelooflijk!

Recipe

Vichyssoise sounds exotic
like the swish of French silk,
insinuating
(like a Cheshire cat)

stakes a claim
like a lover
steaming into a bowl,
an unguent from potatoes, simmered leek,
chicken and salt of bouillon.

After half a century of cooking,
I know words, instructions,
but my favorite recipes comfort
a frightened girl who pushes
her fear hard and fast
swallowing food like junk.

Look, I show her,
the potatoes are friendly when you help them
take off their brown jackets.
They are the ones who give their innards
to make velvet.
Vichyssoise
a promise about working with food,
combining ingredients just so,
to nourish and heal.

The Word of the Day

scro bic u late: having many small
grooves; furrowed
spells scour/bake; it rhymes: you're late
sounds like crows, skewers, all that's scraped

a four-syll-battle cry that ends with ATE
as in consumed, as in greedy as in abominate
accelerate, confiscate, asphyxiate,

as in what we break, but do not plough
as in what we hate but still allow as in
land-rape, scape-goat, throat-cloak,
bloat until scope inflates, as in I had

a dream, a poem, a word (in a word) made
for planting—
                                      a new word to a-
light, yes, we're waiting for a furrowed word
that moves L from the loud clack of cloud
to the soft strummed could.

All of this written because of one word.

Teal in Spring

Teal I see you, teal, as if a lake contains you, again—
not a banner nor the drake
                                eyes ringed with teal.

In morning, you mist into light, drizzle with rain,
reflecting in each drop light knelled
                                with coral and teal.

You are free from ice, alive in frog-dropped splash,
peepers' peal, robin call, a greenish symphony
                                of sound and teal.

You are magic key lifting a fiddlehead ring, shake of blossom.
apple snow and cherry sweep, in a sky
                                more azure than teal.

How you stir the fox kit's heart, as he leaves the birthing den
ready now to thread his long red tale through the woods
                                dappled with teal.

About the author:
Kitty Jospé is a teacher, docent and writer with the code word "enthusiasm" to bring out the inner spark in others. After retiring from teaching French, she continues to teach, giving talks which combine her love of language, art, dance, music, theatre. Since 2008, she has offered a weekly class in poetry appreciation which has a large following.
MA, French Literature: 1984, New York University, NY;
MFA, Creative Writing Poetry, 2009, Pacific University, OR.
Her first book, *Cadences* is available from Foothills Publishing, http://www.foothillspublishing.com/2010/id51.htm

She is thrilled to work with Mary Louise Gerek. *Teal in Spring* started as a ghazal, which inspired the art quilt. The collaboration produced many versions of the poem.
Both quilt and poem as it appears in **Mosaicq** were displayed in the show, *Winter's End*—February 28 to March 30, 2013, Lower Mill Gallery, Honeoye Falls, NY.

About the Cover Artist: Mary Louise Gerek
www.mlfiberarts.com
Mary Louise Gerek has been involved in needle arts as long as she can remember. After 35 years of knitting, spinning, needlepoint and embroidery, she started quilting in 2005, inspired by a trip to the American Southwest.

Her fascination with art quilts and design moved her quickly away from traditional patterns and into the world of creating original pieces. She is intrigued with the effects of fabric manipulation, interaction of color and free motion quilting in her designs.

Teal Spring is her first collaboration with another artist, and she is thrilled with the result. Mary Louise is honored to have worked with Kitty Jospé and have *Teal Spring* as the cover of MOSAICQ.